Magic, Myth, and Mystery

FAIRIES

DO YOU BELIEVE?

This series features creatures that excite our minds. They're magical. They're mythical. They're mysterious. They're also not real. They live in our stories. They're brought to life by our imaginations. Facts about these creatures are based on folklore, legends, and beliefs. We have a rich history of believing in the impossible. But these creatures only live in fantasies and dreams. Monsters do not live under our beds. They live in our heads!

45th Parallel Press

Published in the United States of America by Cherry Lake Publishing
Ann Arbor, Michigan
www.cherrylakepublishing.com

Reading Adviser: Marla Conn MS, Ed., Literacy specialist, Read-Ability, Inc.
Book Design: Felicia Macheske

Photo Credits: © coka/Shutterstock.com, cover; © anat chant/Shutterstock.com, cover; © tomertu/Shutterstock.com, 1; © Slava Gerj/Shutterstock.com, 5; © Triff/Shutterstock.com, 7; © Stepan Kapl/Shutterstock.com, 8; © Fernando Cortes/Shutterstock.com, 11; © conrado/Shutterstock.com, 12; © Uliya Krakos/Shutterstock.com, 15; © Annette Shaff/Shutterstock.com, 17; © boscorelli/Shutterstock.com, 17; © Fly_dragonfly/Shutterstock.com, 18; © Robyn330/Shutterstock.com, 21; © Lia Koltyrina/Shutterstock.com, 22; © Kiselev Andrey Valerevich/Shutterstock.com, 24; © kikujungboy/Shutterstock.com, 27; © Petrenko Andriy/Shutterstock.com, 29

Graphic Elements Throughout: © denniro/Shutterstock.com; © Libellule/Shutterstock.com; © sociologas/Shutterstock.com; © paprika/Shutterstock.com; © ilolab/Shutterstock.com; © Bruce Rolff/Shutterstock.com

45th Parallel Press is an imprint of Cherry Lake Publishing.

Library of Congress Cataloging-in-Publication Data

Names: Loh-Hagan, Virginia, author.
Title: Fairies / by Virginia Loh-Hagan.
Description: Ann Arbor : Cherry Lake Publishing, 2017. | Series: Magic, myth, and mystery | Includes bibliographical references and index.
Identifiers: LCCN 2016031783| ISBN 9781634721479 (hardcover) | ISBN 9781634722131 (pdf) | ISBN 9781634722797 (pbk.) | ISBN 9781634723459 (ebook)
Subjects: LCSH: Fairies—Juvenile literature.
Classification: LCC BF1552 .L64 2017 | DDC 398.21—dc23
LC record available at https://lccn.loc.gov/2016031783

Cherry Lake Publishing would like to acknowledge the work of The Partnership for 21st Century Skills. Please visit *www.p21.org* for more information.

Printed in the United States of America
Corporate Graphics

TABLE of CONTENTS

Believing in Magic

What are fairies? What do fairies look like? How do they interact with humans?

"Do you believe in fairies? If you believe, clap your hands." J. M. Barrie wrote *Peter Pan*. He created Tinker Bell. Tinker Bell is a fairy. She fixes pots. She's a **tinker** of the fairies. Tinker means to fix. She sounds like a tinkling bell. Tinker Bell is like many fairies. She does good things. She does bad things.

Fairies are magical creatures. They're spirits. They're **supernatural**. They're beyond the laws of nature. Some control **fate**. Fate is the things that happen to a person.

Fairies used to live among humans. This is when humans believed in magic. Then humans started believing in religion. Christianity said fairies were evil angels. So, fairies hid. But they're still here. They live all around us.

Fairies are part of European folklore.

Explained by Science!

Bioluminescence is when living creatures make light. Some animals have special chemicals in their bodies. These chemicals combine. They react with oxygen or air. They release light energy. The light is a "cold light." This means it doesn't make heat. Bioluminescence helps animals survive. Some animals use it to camouflage. They blend in with their surroundings. Some animals use it to lure prey. Some use it to signal to others. They signal to mate. They signal to warn. Some animals use it to defend themselves. The light startles predators. It distracts them. Many deep-sea animals have bioluminescence. They live in total darkness. They need to make light to see. They mainly make blue or green lights. Few animals can glow in more than one color. It looks magical when animals make lights. But it's not magic. It's science.

Fairies can look human. But they're not. Some are much smaller. Some are giants. Some have wings. Some are beautiful. Some are ugly. Some make light. Some have fairy dust. There are many different types of fairies.

All fairies have magical powers. Some fairies practice **dark magic**. This is bad magic. Some fairies practice **light magic**. This is good magic. Fairies can be good. They can be bad. They can be both.

Fairies play **pranks** on humans. Pranks are tricks. Some pranks are harmless. Some pranks are dangerous.

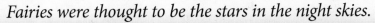

Fairies were thought to be the stars in the night skies.

Fairies interact with humans in different ways. They test humans. They change into beggars. They see if humans will help them. They reward helpful humans. They punish unhelpful humans.

Sometimes fairies help humans. Then, humans have to repay them. Some fairies force humans to hire them. Others force humans to work for them. Then, the humans and fairies are bonded. Once this happens, fairies are hard to get rid of.

Fairies cause **mischief**. Mischief is trouble. Fairies use humans as entertainment. They want attention.

Some humans try to capture fairies. They want fairy treasures. Fairies don't like to be tricked. They'll get even.

Some fairies live together.
Solitary fairies live alone.

Chapter Two

Pixie Powers

How do fairies use their powers for evil? How do they use their powers for good?

Fairies can be dangerous. Some fairies are like vampires. They hunt humans. They drink humans' blood. They turn humans into slaves.

Fairy rings are circles. They're special places to fairies. Fairies dance in them. Humans step in these rings. They do it by accident. Fairies don't like this. They punish humans. They make them dance forever. Humans die from being tired.

Fairies trick humans. They give them **nectar**. Nectar is like a honey drink. Once humans drink, they can never escape. Fairies like to tangle hair of sleeping humans. These tangles are called **elf-locks**. Fairies sometimes steal humans' things.

Fairies are immortal. They live forever.

Humans have life changes. Examples are getting married or having children. Humans are most vulnerable to fairy attacks at this time.

The most common fairy crime is stealing newborns. They replace them with **changelings**. Changelings are fairy children. They're sick. They're deformed.

Fairies also kidnap brides. They kidnap new mothers. They replace them with fairy women. The fairy women trick the human men.

Some humans suddenly die. It's believed that fairies kidnapped them. They replace them with **corpses**. Corpses are dead bodies. Fairies also like to drown humans.

New brides are in danger of fairy attacks.

When Fantasy Meets Reality!

Fireflies are nature's fairy lights. They're also called lightning bugs. Fireflies light up forests at night. Some people think fireflies are fairies. There are many firefly species. Species are animal groups. Each species has its own glow. Their lower stomachs make light. They have their own flashing codes. They flash at each other. They attract prey. They attract mates. One particular species is like bad fairies. It's called Photuris. The females have a trick. They copy flashing codes of other species. They invite males to meet them. They trap them. Then, they eat them. Firefly larvae are called glowworms. Their glow warns predators. They don't taste good. They're poisonous. Fireflies make lights that are yellow, green, or pale red.

Fairies can change into different animals to suit their needs.

But fairies can be kind. They heal humans. They give gifts. They give knowledge. They give blessings.

Fairies weave and spin. They change fate this way. They control what happens. They control luck. They see the future.

They can change into animals. It's common for them to be white deer. They can also talk to animals.

They create **illusions**. Illusions are when things look like things they're not. It's common for them to turn rocks into gold.

Fairies are **nimble**. They move quickly. They're flexible. They have super senses. Some fairies can fly.

Chapter Three

Fairy Fumbles

What are fairies' weaknesses?
Where do fairies live?

Fairies don't like iron. If they touch iron, they can die. Iron makes them back off. It feels like walking on broken glass. To them it smells like rotten eggs. Fairies can be kept in iron cages. Iron stops their magic.

Fairies love sparkly things. They get easily distracted. This gives humans time to run away.

Fairies don't like bread. Bread is connected to homes. It's connected to the taming of nature.

Humans can carry bread in their pockets. They can pour a circle of salt around themselves. Both of these protect them from fairies.

Fairies can't use their powers on other fairies.

Don't let fairies comb your hair.

Fairies live among humans. But they don't like to be seen. They make themselves invisible. They appear. They disappear. They do this quickly. They feel weak when humans see them.

Fairies can travel across **realms**. Realms are worlds. They travel to fairy world. Fairy world is dangerous. It's magical.

Fairies can trap humans in fairy world. They invite humans. They offer humans food. If humans accept the food, they get stuck. They're forced to live like ghosts. They're forced to be slaves. They'll never be happy again. They lose time. One fairy day can equal 100 human years.

SURVIVAL TIPS!

- Never say you don't believe in fairies. A fairy will die. And other fairies will punish you.

- Don't say you're smarter than fairies. Fairies are easily offended. They will prove you wrong.

- Be kind and moral. Fairies enforce morality. They hate people who are greedy, mean, and lazy.

- Follow rules. House fairies are very strict about their rules.

- Avoid entering fairies' homes. Sometimes, fairies' home are bulldozed to build human buildings or roads. Stay away from these places. Fairies will haunt you.

- Don't accept any gifts or favors from fairies. They will want something in return. Accepting fairy magic is dangerous.

- Don't drink or eat anything from the fairy world. You'll be stuck in the fairy world. The fairy world will steal years from your life.

- Know the names of fairies. Calling a fairy by name gives you control.

Chapter Four

Fairies and Beyond

What are some ideas of how fairies originated? What are the different types of fairies?

No one really knows how fairies are born. But there are some ideas.

Some people believe fairies were humans. These humans got lost in fairy world. Over time, magic stuck to their souls. They became fairies.

Some people believe in **faelings**. Faelings are babies. They have one fairy parent. They have one human parent. If a faeling is born in fairy world, he becomes a fairy. If a faeling is born in the human world, he becomes human and never knows he is part fairy.

Some people believe living things have souls. Sometimes these souls become free from these things. These free souls become fairies.

Humans and fairies can have babies together.

Some think fairies are born from **elements**. Elements are earth, water, air, and fire. The elements make up all things.

Earth fairies wander on land. They focus on roots. They work with plants. They work with trees. They work with nature. They wear a lot of green.

Water fairies are also called undines. They live by water. Most of them are female. They lack souls. They marry humans to get souls.

Air fairies are also called sylphs. They float in air. They're invisible. They move toward light. They gather light.

Fire fairies are also called **salamanders**. They bring warmth. They bring heat. They make fire. They make lightning. They create passion.

Flower fairies are popular and based on elements.

Know the Lingo!

- **Asrai:** beautiful female water fairies that melt away into a pool of water when captured or exposed to sunlight

- **Ballybog:** ugly, mud-covered fairies that guard the bogs of Ireland

- **Boggart:** brownies that have turned evil

- **Brownie:** helpful fairies who trade chores for food

- **Fair family or fair folk:** Welsh names for fairies

- **Good neighbors:** common Scottish and Irish name for fairies

- **Green children:** reference to fairies used in medieval stories

- **Old people:** Cornish name for the fairies

- **People in the hills:** fairies that live under the green mounds all over England

- **Pigsies:** another word for pixies

- **Silent moving folk:** Scottish fairies that live in green knolls and mountains

- **Sprite:** elf fairy

- **Wee folk:** Scottish and Irish name for the fairies

There are all types of fairies. Fairies can include other magical creatures.

Elves are beautiful. They love to party. They kidnap humans who listen to their music. They help others.

Pixies are small. They have wings. They're tricksters. They're green. They have a king, queen, and court.

Brownies are males. They have brown skin. They wear brown clothes. They visit houses. They do chores while humans sleep. They want a bowl of cream in return.

Dwarves are old. They turn to stone in daylight. They have deformed feet.

Gnomes have beards. They have white hair. They wear pointed hats. They live in forests. They guard hidden treasures.

Other fairies include leprechauns, trolls, and goblins.

Chapter Five

Tales of Fairies

What are some stories about fairies? What are the Sluagh? Who is Morgan Le Fay?

Irish and Scottish stories feature the Sluagh. They're fairy hosts. They're more feared than death. They're the spirits of the restless dead.

They preyed on humans. They ate their souls. They hid in dark places. They waited for night. Then, they came out. They flew in groups. They looked like flying ravens. They flapped their wings. They screeched.

They entered dying people's houses. They took their souls. Souls were doomed. They became Sluagh. There was no escape. It was easier to steal dying souls. But the Sluagh also hunted living souls.

Nightmares were memories of living souls fighting off the Sluagh.

Real-World Connection

Melynda Moon believes she's from a different realm. She believes she was a fairy in a previous life. She has elf ears. Her ears are pointy. She designed her ears to look like characters from *The Lord of the Rings*. She had an operation. She skinned off the tops of her ears. She cut off the tips of her ears. She formed points. The operation took two hours. She wore stitches for a couple of weeks. Her skin had to join together. Moon loves elves. She thinks they're free spirits. She's been obsessed with mythical things since childhood. She said, "I have always had fantasies about what it would be like to be something other than human. So, I decided to change my appearance to look supernatural. Now I will never go back to being human. I just lack the glitter and wings to fly."

Morgan Le Fay was the queen of fairies. Her name means "Morgan the Fairy." She transformed into a woman. She practiced dark magic. She had many powers. She could raise the dead. She commanded monsters and evil spirits. She knew more spells than any other fairy. She could change shapes. She could fly. But she wasn't totally evil. She was also a healer.

Le Fay was from Avalon in England. She was beautiful. She was related to King Arthur. She helped heal him. Then, she became his enemy. She helped cause his death.

Fairies come in all shapes and sizes. Beware!

Some people thought Morgan Le Fay was a witch.

Did You Know?

- The word *fairy* comes from the Latin word *fata*. Fata means fate.

- Some people in Ireland built fairy paths in their houses. They built their front and back doors directly opposite each other. They left doors open. This allowed fairies to travel through the house.

- Some people confuse angels and fairies. Angels are messengers of God. They're part of Christian stories. Fairies are part of folk stories. They live among humans.

- Fairies have a lot of power on Halloween night. Some parents in Ireland used to put oatmeal and salt in their children's hair to ward off fairies on Halloween.

- Sometimes mushrooms grow in a circle. These circles are called fairy rings. They're found in forests. Some people believed they were paths made by dancing fairies.

- Ly Erg is a Scottish fairy. He's small. He's dressed like a soldier. He has a red hand. The red is blood. When people fight him, they die in two weeks.

- Muryans were Cornish fairies. They had bad souls. They used to be humans. They did bad deeds. They got smaller and smaller. They became the size of ants. It became bad luck to attack anthills.

- Will O' the Wisp are balls of light. They're seen over swamps. Some people think they're dancing fairies. Other people think they're the souls of dead children.

Consider This!

Take a Position: Read the 45th Parallel Press book about witches. Some people believe fairies are witches. Do you agree or disagree with this thinking? Argue your point with reasons and evidence.

Say What? Fairies can be good and bad. Explain how fairies can be light. Explain how they can be dark.

Think About It! Today's fairies are nice and pretty. They do good deeds. But most fairies from the past are mean. They do bad deeds. Why do you think today's stories about fairies are different from past stories?

Learn More

- Marriott, Susannah. *A Field Guide to Fairies: Explore the Secret World of the Fairy Realm*. Hauppauge, NY: Barron's Educational Series, 2009.

- Moorey, Teresa. *The Fairy Bible: Everything You Ever Wanted to Know About Fairies*. New York: Sterling, 2008.

- Reinhart, Matthew, and Robert Sabuda. *Fairies and Magical Creatures*. Somerville, MA: Candlewick, 2008.

Glossary

changelings (CHAYNJ-lingz) fairy children that replace kidnapped human children

corpses (KORPS-iz) dead bodies

dark magic (DAHRK MAJ-ik) bad magic

elements (EL-uh-muhnts) earth, water, air, and fire

elf-locks (ELF-lahks) tangled hair

faelings (FAY-lingz) the babies of a human and fairy

fate (FAYT) the things that happen to a person

illusions (ih-LOO-zhuhnz) deceptive appearances

light magic (LITE MAJ-ik) good magic

mischief (MIS-chif) trouble

nectar (NEK-tur) sweet juice from plants

nimble (NIM-buhl) quick or agile

pranks (PRANGKS) tricks

realms (RELMZ) worlds, lands, or dimensions

salamanders (SAL-uh-man-durz) fire fairies

supernatural (soo-pur-NACH-ur-uhl) beyond the laws of nature

tinker (TING-kur) a fixer of things

Index

About the Author

Dr. Virginia Loh-Hagan is an author, university professor, former classroom teacher, and curriculum designer. She definitely believes in fairies! She lives in San Diego with her very tall husband and very naughty dogs. To learn more about her, visit www.virginialoh.com.